5-Minute Daily Practice

Test Taking

BY JACQUELINE B. GLASTHAL

SCHOLASTIC
PROFESSIONALBOOKS

New York • Toronto • London • Auckland • Sydney • Mexico City
New Delhi • Hong Kong • Buenos Aires

To Roni and Amy—with love.
—JG (a.k.a. Yoey)

Cover design by **Gerard Fuchs**
Cover art by **Dave Clegg**
Interior design by **Holly Grundon**
Interior illustrations by **Mike Moran**

ISBN: 0-439-43112-3
Copyright © 2003 by Jacqueline B. Glasthal
All rights reserved. Published by Scholastic Inc.
Printed in the U.S.A.

2 3 4 5 6 7 8 9 10   40   09 08 07 06 05 04 03

5-Minute Daily Practice

Contents

Introduction

Common Test-Taking Pitfalls

- Not reading carefully—or working too fast—just to get through the test

- Sloppiness, resulting in test graders not being able to read the work

- Neglecting to study, or not using practice tests to improve abilities

- Ignoring the directions and instead going right to the questions

- Spending so much time on one question or section (or writing so neatly), that there is not enough time to complete the test

- "Freezing," due to test phobias

- Answering short-answer and essay questions with the shortest responses possible

- Filling in fill-in-the-blank or multiple choice responses in the wrong spaces

- Forgetting to use a Number 2 pencil

Taking tests in school—and standardized tests in particular—can be difficult. At times, instructions, directions, or questions are phrased in such a way that they will trip a child up—even if he or she reads carefully. Thus, the more experience students have with a variety of test-taking formats and question types, the more prepared they will be for whatever they may face on any kind of test.

By using this book, students will gain practice in all six basic test types: multiple choice, true/false, matching, fill-in-the-blanks, short answer, and essay. I've also varied the phrasing of directions in many cases—and thrown in some unexpected instructions. This will reinforce the importance of reading carefully, and prepare students for the trickier ways questions may appear on their tests.

Preparing Students for "The Real Thing"

As you check over students' work, keep an eye out for the types of errors they tend to make most often. Then, as you go over the answers as a class, discuss strategies that students can rely on to help them avoid common pitfalls. Prompt them with questions such as: *What clues in the instructions helped you figure out what to do? Could you immediately eliminate any wrong answers on the multiple-choice questions? How might you pace yourself so you have time to answer all the questions? What do you think a good short answer to a question includes? How can you keep from getting nervous when taking a test? What tips might help you fill in multiple-choice answers in the right spaces?*

If a number of students answer the same question incorrectly, go over that problem as a group. Allow children to explain why they gave the answer that they did. Did they select as "true" something that is often the case, but does not hold true "always," or "in all cases"? Or was there something about the phrasing of the question that confused everyone?

Many of the problems in this book require students to write their answers on a separate sheet of paper. Remind students to write their name on any pages that you want them to turn in. For additional practice in listening and following directions, instruct children to place their name on the sheets in a very specific way. For example, you might have them write their name at the top of the page and the date at the bottom, their last name first, or put their initials in parentheses.

What Are the Tests Like Near You?

The more familiar you are with your own state's standardized tests, the easier it will be to adapt the prompts suggested here to conform to those given in your district. For example, if students are told to write their answers on a separate sheet, you might reproduce each question on a page that you distribute, along with a separate sheet on which you direct students to write their answers. If you know that children will be given tight time constraints in which to complete each section of your own area's standardized tests, instruct them to keep track of how long it takes them to complete each problem. This will provide a sense of how long it takes them to complete the various question types.

The trick to helping students improve their test-taking and directions-following skills is practice, practice, practice. There's no better way to provide children with the tools—and confidence—to get through even the most stressful test-taking day.

Following Directions

Name: _____

1. What do recipes, street signs, tests at school, model airplane kits, and board games have in common? They all contain written directions that need to be followed.

List five more places where you commonly find written directions. Label them A through E.

> **TiP**
>
> Never begin work until you have read all of the directions first, and you are sure you understand exactly what you are being asked to do.

Following Directions

Name: _____

2. At one time or another, just about everyone has had a problem occur when trying to do something—as a result of not reading the directions carefully first.

List five or more things that might go wrong if you tried to bake a cake without carefully reading all the directions in the recipe first. Feel free to exaggerate the things that can wrong, and make your list as humorous as you like.

Following Directions

Name: _____

3. Parents, teachers, school crossing guards, doctors, beach lifeguards, and Little League coaches are all people who might give you verbal directions that need to be followed.

Write down one example of a direction each of the people listed above might say to you.

Name: _____

Following Directions

4. During an emergency, it is particularly important to follow directions.

List three or more instructions you might be given if you were in a building when a fire alarm went off.

Name: _____

Following Directions

5. What is the procedure you are asked to follow when there is a fire drill at your school?

List the steps you are supposed to take, in order from first to last. Then go over the list with your class to see if there are any steps that you left out.

Name: _____

Following Directions

6. Follow these instructions as precisely as you can.

Draw a square next to a circle and a triangle.
Explain in a sentence or two why there is more than one correct way to follow these directions as they are written.

TiP

When you understand the purpose of a set of directions, there is less chance that you will misinterpret them.

Name: _____

Following Directions

7. Rewrite these directions more precisely so there is only one correct way to follow them.

Draw a square next to a circle and a triangle.
Pass your paper to a classmate. Can he or she accurately follow the directions you wrote?

Name: _____

8. Is there only one way to do the following?

Fold a sheet of paper in half, and then in half again.
List the different ways you can think of that this can be done. Use illustrations, if you'd like, to help explain your thinking.

Name: _____

9. How many ways can you find to color in half of a square, like the one shown here?

Draw similar grids on graph paper. Then color in half of each one in a different way. Use the small squares created by the grid lines to help you. Be as creative as you can!

Name: _____

10. Cross out every other letter in this series to decode a secret message.

DHIODWYDOIUDKYNOOUWKWNHOIWCWHHLIECTHTLEERTTTOECRRTOOSCSROOUSTSFOIURTSFTIHRESRTE?

Compare the message you arrived at with others in your class. Did everyone wind up decoding the exact same message? Discuss with a classmate why all of the messages might not be the same.

Name: _____

11. Imagine you have a robot that will do anything you want it to. However, if your directions aren't precise, you may be surprised at what happens!

Write out a detailed set of "programming instructions" for a robot on how to make a peanut butter and jelly sandwich. Then swap papers with a partner, and compare your sets of instructions. Can you identify any steps the robot might need to do that you and/or your partner left out?

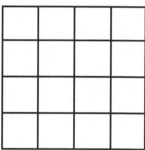

Hint
Remember: The robot will only do exactly what it is told!

Name: _____

12. In each circle, draw a face that expresses a different emotion (such as happy or sad). Beneath each circle, write a word describing the emotion.

◯   ◯   ◯   ◯   ◯

___   ___   ___   ___   ___

Name: _____

13. Beginning with A, put a ✓ in every other circle below.
Fully darken in the remaining circles.

◯   ◯   ◯   ◯   ◯   ◯

A   **B**   **C**   **D**   **E**   **F**

Name: _____

14. Put an **X** in the circles below that are multiples of 9.
Draw a funny face in any remaining circles.

◯   ◯   ◯   ◯   ◯

18   72   129   234   243

Name: _____

15. Put an **X** in the spaces below next to the names of oceans. Put a ✓ in the spaces below next to the names of continents.

◯ Antarctica   ◯ Asia   ◯ Arctic   ◯ North America

◯ Europe   ◯ Pacific   ◯ Australia   ◯ Indian

◯ South America   ◯ Africa   ◯ Atlantic

Following Directions

Name: _____

16. Fill in the space below beside any sentence that does not contain all 26 letters of the alphabet.

a) ◯ My very educated mother just served us nine pizzas.

b) ◯ The quick brown fox jumps over the lazy dog.

c) ◯ A soda jerk explained how fizzy beverages quench my thirst.

d) ◯ Quiet jungle explorers discovered young zebras while making a fire.

Following Directions

Name: _____

17. Create your own sentence that contains all 26 letters of the alphabet. Circle each letter the first time that it appears in the sentence so that when you're done, 26 letters are circled.

Following Directions

Name: _____

18. Imagine you are about to take a standardized test. Your teacher hands out the papers and tells you that you will have exactly 30 minutes to work on it.

If the test begins at exactly 9:12, at what time will she tell you to put down your pencils? Raise your hand when you think you know the answer.

Following Directions

Name: _____

19. Imagine you are about to take a standardized test. Your teacher hands out the papers and tells you that you will have exactly 50 minutes to work on it.

If the test begins at exactly 9:48, at what time will she tell you to put down your pencils? Put your head down on your desk when you think you know the answer.

Name: _____

20. Carefully study the diagrams below, which show different ways to loop a piece of yarn, twine, string, or rope. Circle the ones that you believe will form a knot when both ends are pulled.

a) 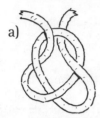   b) 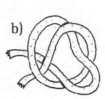   c) 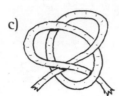   d) 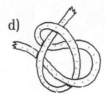   e)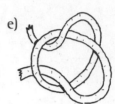

Name: _____

21. Loop a piece of yarn, twine, string, or rope that is at least 18 inches long, to form each shape below. Pull on each end to find out if you've made a knot—or not! Put a square around each one that forms a knot when you pull on both ends.

a) 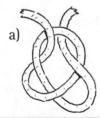   b) 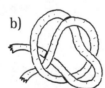   c) 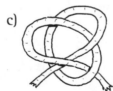   d) 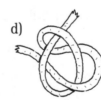   e)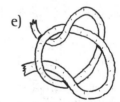

Name: _____

22. Using a pair of scissors, and a square sheet of paper that is at least 9" x 9", follow the directions below.

A. Fold the sheet diagonally to create a triangle shape.

B. Fold up one corner of the base to meet the top point. Repeat for the opposite corner.

C. Fold the entire shape in half, vertically.

D. Cut away the bottom of the folded shape at a diagonal.

E. Unfold the paper. Write a description of the result you see.

Name: _____

23. Read and follow this set of instructions. Be sure to read them all the way through before you begin.

A. Write your name in the upper right-hand corner of a separate sheet of paper.

B. Write the date in the upper left corner of the same page.

C. Write the total number of questions on this paper just beneath the date.

D. Beneath the total number of questions on this paper, write the total number of siblings (brothers and sisters) you have.

E. Write the alphabet along the bottom of the page, starting with A in the lower right-hand corner, moving toward Z in the lower left-hand corner.

F. Fold your paper in half lengthwise, so you can't read what you wrote.

G. Stand up and stretch. Then bend over and touch your toes.

H. Walk around your chair three times, counter-clockwise.

I. Do 12 jumping jacks.

J. Pat your head and rub your belly at the same time. Then sit down.

K. Hand your paper in to your teacher.

L. Only follow steps A, B, and L.

Name: _____

24. In the spaces below, place the numbers 1 to 9 to indicate the order of the planets, in terms of nearness to the sun.

○ Pluto   ○ Earth   ○ Mercury

○ Mars   ○ Saturn   ○ Uranus

○ Jupiter   ○ Venus   ○ Neptune

TiP

When asked to sequence a group of items, be sure it's clear in what order these items should be listed (for example: smallest to largest).

Name: _____

Sequencing

25. Place a number from **1** to **9** in each space below to create a mnemonic sentence that helps you remember the order of the planets, in terms of nearness to the sun.

○ My   ○ Pizzas   ○ Us

○ Served   ○ Just   ○ Educated

○ Nine   ○ Mother   ○ Very

TiP

A *mnemonic*, or memory jogger, is a sentence or phrase to help you remember something.

Name: _____

Sequencing

26. Create your own mnemonic to help you remember the order of the planets, in terms of nearness to the sun.

Name: _____

Sequencing

27. Create two mnemonic sentences: one to help you remember Earth's seven continents and the other to help you remember its four oceans. Label the page to help you remember what the mnemonics represent.

Name: _____

Sequencing

28. In correct order, the colors of the rainbow are Red, Orange, Yellow, Green, Blue, Indigo, and Violet.

Entering only one letter in each circle below, write the *acronym* (the name or word made from the first letter or letters in a series or phrase) that many people use to help them remember this sequence.

○ ○ ○ ○ ○ . ○ ○ ○

Name: _____

29. **Arrange these words in order.**

Write number **1** next to the shortest time period listed, **2** next to the next-shortest time period listed, and so on—until you place number **10** next to the longest time period.

Hour _____   Week _____

Year _____   Second _____

Decade _____   Day _____

Month _____   Millisecond _____

Century _____   Minute _____

Name: _____

30. **Arrange these words in order.**

Place a tally mark (/) next to the time period that takes place most often, two tally marks (//) next to the time period that takes place next most often, and so on—until you place nine tally marks (卌 ////) next to the time period that occurs least frequently.

Hint

Five tally marks look like this: 卌

Annually _____   Semiannually _____

Quarterly _____   Centennially _____

Millennially _____   Semiweekly _____

Weekly _____   Daily _____

Monthly _____

Name: _____

31. Arrange these words in numerical order.

Write A next to the largest multiple birth, B next to the next-smallest multiple birth, and so on—until you place I next to the smallest multiple birth listed.

Quadruplets _____   Nonuplets _____

Decaplets _____   Quintuplets _____

Septuplets _____   Twins _____

Sextuplets _____   Triplets _____

Octuplets _____

Name: _____

32. Arrange these words in numerical order.

Write A next to the shape that has the fewest number of angles, B next to the shape that has the second fewest number of angles, and so on—until you place J next to the shape that has more angles than any of the other shapes listed.

Decagon _____   Dodecagon _____

Triangle _____   Quadrilateral _____

Pentagon _____   Octagon _____

Hendecagon _____   Nonagon _____

Hexagon _____   Heptagon _____

Name: _____

33.   Arrange these words in numerical order.

Write the number **1** next to the word that means "first," **2** next to the word meaning "second," and so on—until you place **10** next to the word meaning "tenth."

Quaternary   _____   Denary   _____

Septenary   _____   Secondary   _____

Quinary   _____   Nonary   _____

Tertiary   _____   Primary   _____

Octonary   _____   Senary   _____

Name: _____

34.   What do you think each of the following prefixes means?

Tri- _____   Quad- _____   Oct- _____

Deca- _____   Cent- _____

Hint

Think of other words that contain these word parts to help you figure them out.

Name: _____

35.   Order the following amounts from least to greatest, using the numbers 1 to 4.

◯   4 teaspoons   ◯   1 ounce

◯   1 tablespoon   ◯ $\frac{1}{2}$ cup

Hint

3 teaspoons = 1 tablespoon

2 tablespoons = 1 ounce

8 fluid ounces = 1 cup

Name: _____

Sequencing

36. Order the following amounts from least to greatest, using the letters A to D. On a separate sheet of paper, explain your thinking.

○ $1\frac{1}{2}$ cups   ○ 14 ounces

○ $\frac{3}{4}$ quart   ○ $\frac{1}{2}$ pint

Hint

1 cup = 8 fluid ounces
2 cups = 1 pint
2 pints = 1 quart

Name: _____

Sequencing

37. Order the following lengths from longest to shortest, using the Roman numerals I to IV.

○ $2\frac{1}{2}$ feet   ○ $\frac{1}{8}$ mile

○ 40 inches   ○ 4 yards

Hint

12 inches = 1 foot
3 feet = 1 yard
1,760 yards = 1 mile

Name: _____

Sequencing

38. Rewrite the following metric prefixes in order from largest to smallest. Write the meaning of the prefix next to each.

Centi-   Milli-   Deca-

Kilo-   Hecto-   Deci-

Hint

If necessary, use a dictionary or other reference book to help you.

Name: _____

Sequencing

39. Write a description of the pattern that was used to create the following number sequence. Below, provide the next three numbers that continue the pattern.

| $\frac{1}{2}$ | $\frac{2}{4}$ | $\frac{3}{6}$ | $\frac{4}{8}$ | $\frac{5}{10}$ | | | |

Name: _____

40. Write a description of the pattern that was used to create the following number sequence. Below, provide the next three numbers that continue the pattern.

| 2 | 6 | 12 | 20 | 30 | | | |

Name: _____

41. Write a description of the pattern that was used to create the following number sequence. Below, provide the next three numbers that continue the pattern.

| 1 | 4 | 9 | 16 | 25 | | | |

Name: _____

42. Create a time line that shows at least one significant event that has occurred during each year of your life. The event can be something that was especially important to you, your family, or the world.

Name: _____

43. What is the number of oranges needed to make one quart of pure fresh-squeezed orange juice?

Write your *estimate*, along with a short paragraph explaining how you arrived at it.

Hint
Usually, three medium oranges, weighing a total of about 1 pound, yield 8 ounces of juice.

Name: _____

44. Draw a line from each metric unit listed below to the item, of those listed, that it would most likely be used to describe.

TiP

When you first receive a test, try to estimate how much time you will need to allot to each section. Be sure that you don't spend too much time on one question.

Milliliter	A bottle of soda
Gram	The width of a fingernail
Kilogram	A grain of sand
Kilometer	A teaspoon of water
Liter	The length of a baseball bat
Milligram	A dollar bill
Millimeter	The thickness of a penny
Centimeter	An airport landing strip
Meter	A sack of oranges

Name: _____

45. Estimate the metric measurement of each of the following items. Explain your thinking in a sentence or two beside each estimate.

a) The length of a pencil
b) The weight of a grapefruit
c) The volume of a mug of hot chocolate

Name: _____

46. Estimate about how many times in 60 seconds you think you can . . .

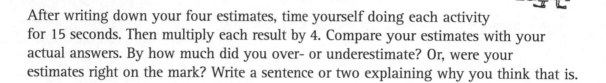

Mississippi

a) touch your toes.   b) clap your hands.

c) write your name.   d) say "Mississippi."

After writing down your four estimates, time yourself doing each activity for 15 seconds. Then multiply each result by 4. Compare your estimates with your actual answers. By how much did you over- or underestimate? Or, were your estimates right on the mark? Write a sentence or two explaining why you think that is.

Name: _____

47. Of the shapes below, which ones do you think could be made into a cube if they were cut out and folded along the dotted lines? Circle the letter next to each of those shapes. In a written description, tell what these shapes all have in common. Finally, draw another shape that has these properties, and that you think can be folded into a cube.

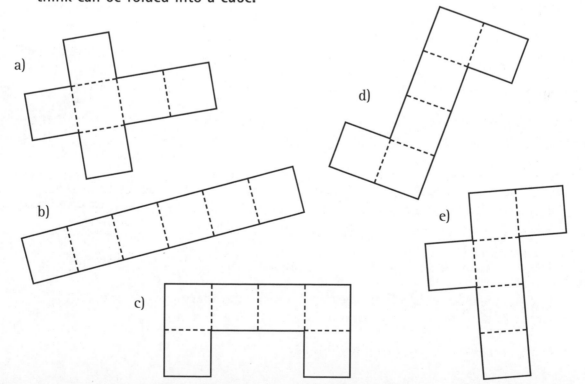

Name: _____

48. A *prefix* is a word part that comes at the beginning of a word that helps to determine that word's meaning.

The prefix *micro-* implies something very small. Words that begin with this prefix include *microscope, microwave, microbe, microcosm,* and *microfilm.* Write these words in alphabetical order, and define each one.

TiP

Use prefixes and suffixes for clues as to what an unfamiliar word means.

Name: _____

49. A *suffix* is a word part that comes at the end of a word that helps to determine that word's meaning.

The suffix *-logy* means "a science," or "the study of." Words that end with this suffix include *ecology, biology, technology, criminology,* and *genealogy.* Write these words in alphabetical order, and define each one.

Hint

Try to do this without using a dictionary.

Name: _____

50. The prefix *pre-* means "before."

List five or more words that begin with this prefix. Place the words in alphabetical order, and use each one in a sentence.

Name: _____

51. The prefix *un-* means "not," or "the opposite of."

List five or more words that begin with this prefix. Place the words in alphabetical order, and use each one in a sentence.

Name: _____

Vocabulary

52. The suffix *–ment* implies a concrete result or action.

List five or more words that end in this suffix. Place the words in alphabetical order, and use each one in a sentence.

Name: _____

Vocabulary

53. The suffix *–ship* implies a state, condition, or quality.

List five or more words that end in this suffix. Place the words in alphabetical order, and use each one in a sentence.

Name: _____

Vocabulary

54. Put an X through the word below that is not a synonym for the word *little*. Write a definition for it, and use it in a sentence.

tiny   small   minute
paltry   slight   considerable

Hint

If necessary, use a dictionary to help you.

Name: _____

Vocabulary

55. List three or more words that are synonyms for *said*. Place them in alphabetical order, and use each one in a sentence.

Name: _____

Vocabulary

56. Put an X through the word below that is not an antonym for the word *hot*. Write a definition for it, and use it in a sentence.

freezing   cold   tepid
icy   chilly   frosty

Hint

If necessary, use a dictionary to help you.

Name: _____

Vocabulary

57. List three or more words that are antonyms for *slow*. Place them in alphabetical order, and use each one in a sentence.

Name: _____

Vocabulary

58. Rewrite the following sentence using simpler words.

The gourmand was contrite, and pledged to be abstemious when admonished for his intemperance and voracious appetite.

TiP

Sometimes studying how a word is used in context can help you figure out its meaning.

Name: _____

Vocabulary

59. Rewrite the following sentence using simpler words.

Sheldon was flabbergasted at his curmudgeonly grandmother's vociferous complaints over Sheldon's facetious banter.

TiP

Seeing a familiar word within a longer word can sometimes help you decode the longer word's meaning.

Name: _____

60. Are you a *sesquipedalian*? That's someone who likes to use overly long words. If you are, you might be interested to know the longest unhyphenated word recognized by most English language dictionaries:

Pneumonoultramicroscopicsilicovolcanoconiosis

That's a mouthful, huh? It refers to a lung disease that comes from inhaling very fine particles of silicate or quartz dust. To help you understand how this word came to be, draw a line from each part of this word (given on the left) to its correct meaning, from the choices given, on the right.

pneumo	referring to particles found in a volcano
ultra-microscopic	silicon-related
silico	lung
volcano	diseased condition
coni	extra small
osis	dust

TiP

Think of other words you know that contain the same, or similar, word parts.

Name: _____

61. The following words, when unscrambled, relate to weather. Unscramble and define each one.

a) Z D R L E I Z   b) D S O U L C   b) N A I R   d) N W D I

Name: _____

62. Which word given below does not belong in the set? Circle it, and write a sentence or two explaining what the others have in common that this word does not.

apiary   aviary   estuary
cage   aquarium   sanctuary

Hint

If necessary, use a dictionary to help you.

Vocabulary

Name: _____

63. Six simple machines are described below. Each one makes some types of work easier by helping the people using it to push or pull a load. Read the descriptions. Then match each one with an example of that type of tool. Draw a line between them.

a) **inclined plane:** A flat surface, such as a piece of wood, that is inclined, or slanted, in such a way as to help move an object. The longer the slope of the inclined plane, the easier it is to pull or push the heavy object up the inclined plane.

b) **lever:** A tool that pries something loose.

c) **pulley:** A simple machine that uses grooved wheels and a rope to raise, lower, or move a load.

d) **screw:** An inclined plane wrapped around a cylinder, giving it a sharp edge which helps it hold things together or lift materials.

e) **wedge:** The pointed edge of an inclined plane, used to push things apart, or keep things in place.

f) **wheel and axle:** A circular frame, which turns a rod, crank, or handle attached to its center, helping it to lift or move loads.

Vocabulary

Name: _____

64. Explain in your own words what distinguishes the six types of simple machines from each other (inclined plane, lever, pulley, screw, wedge, and wheel and axle). Then name and illustrate another example of each. Note that your examples should be different than those shown in #63.

Name: _____

65. *Homonyms* are two or more words that sound the same when spoken aloud, though their meanings (and sometimes their spellings) are different.

In the silly rhyme that follows, find and underline the homonym pair that appears in each line of the poem. (The first one is done for you.)

An Ode To Homonyms

Do you <u>see</u> the <u>sea</u>?

Would you like to be a bee?

Here is the ode I owed you.

In it, you'll read a silly rhyme or two, too.

You'll find a king who's thrown from his throne.

And meet a banker, who takes out a lone loan,

You'll get to know the doctor with patience for patients.

She's here among the others, do you hear?

We're all living as residents in our residence.

This, to me, makes good dollar-and-cents sense!

Name: _____

66. Find five or more words in the silly poem "An Ode to Homonyms" (that you have not already underlined in #65) for which you can think of a homonym match. Circle these words. Then write each word and its homonym match.

Name: _____

67. Think of five or more homonym word pairs that do not appear in the poem "An Ode to Homonyms," and list them.

Name: _____

68. Create your own silly poem or paragraph using three or more homonym word pairs that do not appear in the poem "An Ode to Homonyms."

Name: _____

69. When two words with the exact same spelling have entirely different meanings, those words are referred to as *homographs*.

Write two sentences for each homograph, each one incorporating a different meaning of the word. Explain what one meaning of each of these words all have in common.

Homographs	
bat	plate
coach	uniform
field	strike
pen	base

Name: _____

70. In a sentence or two, sum up the similarities and differences between homonyms and homographs.

Name: _____

71. Using a dictionary, look up the meanings of the words listed below. Then use what you learn to label this diagram of a leaf correctly.

a) apex

b) lower epidermis

c) margin

d) midrib

e) stem

f) upper epidermis

g) veins

Name: _____

72. In the following sentence, some of the words are spelled incorrectly. Rewrite the sentence, spelling all of the words correctly.

You're absense was soarly mised at the skool's holliday celebrashun yesterday.

TiP

If a word doesn't look right to you when you see it on the page, try an alternate spelling to see if that looks better.

Spelling

Name: _____

73. In the following sentence, some of the words are spelled incorrectly. Rewrite only the misspelled words, spelling each of them correctly.

Our local sherrif gave a fassinating talk about the American legle system.

Spelling

Name: _____

74. In a *rebus*, a combination of pictures, symbols, letters, and numbers are used to represent words. Decipher the following rebus sentences. Rewrite the sentences, spelling out all of the words correctly, and using correct punctuation.

B + + DAY.   TH +

Spelling

Name: _____

75. Create an original rebus sentence. Then trade with a partner to see if you can decipher each other's rebus sentences. When deciphering your partner's rebus sentence, be sure to spell out all the words correctly, and use the correct punctuation.

Spelling

Name: _____

76. To begin, one student calls out a letter. As you go around the group, each student adds a letter until a word is spelled out.

The goal is *not* to add the last letter that completes the spelling. If you do, you are out. If someone challenges you, arguing that it's impossible to spell out a word given the letter you added, you must be able to prove otherwise. If you can't, you are also out. If you can prove that you did have a word in mind, the person who challenged you is out instead. The last student remaining wins the game.

Do this activity in a small group.

Problem Solving

Name: _____

77. In the following word puzzle, each letter stands for another one in the alphabet. Try to decode it. You may want to create a small chart to help you keep track of the letters. Do you notice a pattern?

TIP
To solve some types of problems, you need to try out a variety of solutions to help you narrow your response down to the correct one.

Hint
In this puzzle the letter J stands for the letter E.

N YJWVZA RGZ FV NMCJ UZ LZAUWFMTUJ VZBJUGFAH UZ UGJ

RZWCK FV N IZWUTANUJ YJWVZA, NAK JNLG ZI TV VGZTCK MJ

NMCJ NU CJNVU UZ "MWFHGUJA UGJ LZWAJW" RGJWJ RJ NWJ.

–LGNWCJV VLGTCUO, LNWUZZAFVU

Problem Solving

Name: _____

78. In the following word puzzle, each letter stands for another one in the alphabet. Try to decode it. You may want to make a small chart to help you keep track of the letters. Once you've deciphered the puzzle, describe the pattern that the letter substitutes form.

Hint

In this puzzle the letter R stands for the letter I.

R SZEV Z WIVZN GSZG LMV WZB GSRH MZGRLM DROO IRHV FK

ZMW OREV LFG GSV GIFV NVZMRMT LU RGH XIVVW: "DV SLOW

GSVHV GIFGSH GL YV HVOU-VERWVMG; GSZG ZOO NVM ZIV

XIVZGVW VJFZO."

–NZIGRM OFGSVI PRMT, QI., XRERO IRTSGH OVZWVI

Problem Solving

Name: _____

79. In the following puzzle, each letter stands for a number.

Use the rules of addition to figure out what number is represented by each letter.

$$
\begin{array}{r}
ONE \\
+\ ONE \\
\hline
TWO
\end{array}
$$

Hint

Begin with the letter O. What is the largest number it can be?

E = _____   N = _____   O = _____   T = _____   W = _____

Name: _____

80. What number belongs in each circle?

To figure it out, look at the numbers written in the boxes between the circles. Combined, the numbers in the two circles that each box touches should add up to that number. Write the correct number solution in each circle.

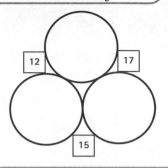

Name: _____

81. Add +, −, x, and/or ÷ symbols and parentheses, if necessary, between the numbers in the following equation so that the equation is true.

$$3 \rule{2cm}{0.4pt} 11 \rule{2cm}{0.4pt} 4 = 36 \rule{2cm}{0.4pt} 1$$

Name: _____

82. Find a number that has a remainder of 6 when divided by 7, and a remainder of 2 when divided by 5. In writing, explain how you arrived at your answer.

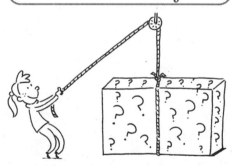

Name: _____

83. Find a number that has a remainder of 2 when divided by 3, a remainder of 3 when divided by 5, and a remainder of 1 when divided by 7.

Multiple Choice

Name: _____

84. A recipe for a batch of 12 chocolate chip cookies calls for $2/3$ cup of chocolate chips. Marcie has 2 cups of chocolate chips. If she adjusts the recipe to use all of the chips she has, how many cookies will she have made when she is done?

Ⓐ 3 cookies   Ⓑ 2 batches

Ⓒ 36 cookies   Ⓓ 36 batches

TiP

When facing a multiple-choice question, narrow down the choices by determining which answers are definitely incorrect.

Multiple Choice

Name: _____

85. Solve the following equation, and explain why you think each wrong answer was included as an option.

$24 \div 6 =$ _____

Ⓐ 144   Ⓑ 4   Ⓒ 18   Ⓓ 30

Multiple Choice

Name: _____

86. Solve the following equation, and explain why you think each wrong answer was included as an option.

$1,029 \div 15 =$ _____

Ⓐ 61   Ⓑ 64   Ⓒ 68 R9   Ⓓ 66 R6

Multiple Choice

Name: _____

87. Solve the following equation, and explain why you think each wrong answer was included as an option.

$325 \times 5 =$ _____

Ⓐ 330   Ⓑ 1,625   Ⓒ 1,595   Ⓓ 1,725

Name: _____

88. Solve the following equation, and explain why you think each wrong answer was included as an option.

157 − 23 = _____

(A) 200   (B) 180   (C) 155   (D) 134

TiP

Be ready for math problems that are written both vertically and horizontally. You never know which way they will be on a test!

Name: _____

89. Solve the following equation, and explain why you think each wrong answer was included as an option.

$2.29 x 5 = _____

(A) 11.45   (B) $10.45   (C) 1,145   (D) $11.45

Name: _____

90. Of the 16 billion U.S. coins produced each year, about $3/4$ are pennies. About how many pennies are produced in the United States each year?

(A) About 12,000,000,000 pennies   (B) About 21,000,000,000 pennies

(C) About 4,000,000,000 pennies   (D) About 5,000,000,000 pennies

Name: _____

91. Note the way these four rows of blocks create a pattern of steps. If you were to add two additional rows to the pattern, how many blocks would the new shape contain in all?

(A) 6 blocks   (B) 10 blocks

(C) 15 blocks   (D) 21 blocks

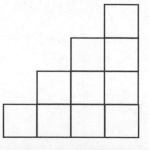

True/False

Name: _____

92. Add parentheses to the following equation so that, when you're done, the equation will be true.

$$5 \times 7 + 4 = 10 \div 2 + 25 \times 2$$

TIP

Be careful when you see the word *always* or *never* on a test. Since there tend to be exceptions to most rules, these answer choices are often wrong!

True/False

Name: _____

93. Determine whether the following statement is true or false. Write *true* or *false* and explain your thinking. Use one or more math problems to back up your argument.

If two numbers are each divisible by a smaller number, their sum is also divisible by that smaller number.

True/False

Name: _____

94. Determine whether the following statement is true or false. Write *true* or *false* and explain your thinking. Use one or more math problems to back up your argument.

If a number is divisible by **9**, it is also divisible by **3**.

Name: _____

95. Determine whether the following statement is true or false. Write *true* or *false* and explain your thinking. Use one or more math problems to back up your argument.

If a number is divisible by 3, it is also divisible by 9.

Name: _____

96. Determine whether the following statement is true or false. Write *true* or *false* and explain your thinking. Use one or more math problems to back up your argument.

If you multiply any number by a number that is divisible by a smaller number, the product is also divisible by the smaller number.

Name: _____

97. Determine whether the following statement is true or false. Write *true* or *false* and explain your thinking. Use one or more math problems to back up your argument.

A good quick tip for dividing by 10 is to move the decimal point in the other number one place to the right.

Name: _____

98. Determine whether the following statement is true or false. Write *true* or *false* and explain your thinking. Use one or more math problems to back up your argument.

A good quick tip for dividing by 5 is to double the other number, and then divide by 10.

Name: _____

99. Fill in the blank in the following sentence with the word or number that will make the sentence true.

All even numbers are divisible by _____.

TiP

Sometimes, if you can visualize what a question is asking, that problem becomes easier to solve.

Name: _____

100. Fill in the blank in the following sentence with the word or number that will make the sentence true.

A number is divisible by 6 if it is divisible by 3 and by 2, if it is even, and if the sum of its digits is divisible by _____.

Name: _____

101. Fill in the blank in the following sentence with the word or number that will make the sentence true.

A number is divisible by _____ if the number formed by the last three digits in the number is divisible by 8.

Name: _____

102. Fill in the blanks in the following sentence with the words or numbers that will make the sentence true.

A number is divisible by _____ if the number formed by the last two digits in the number is divisible by _____.

Name: _____

103. Fill in the blank in the following sentence with the word or number that will make the sentence true.

A good shortcut for multiplying by 5 is to multiply by 10 and then divide by _____ .

Name: _____

104. Fill in the blank in the following sentence with the word or number that will make it true.

A good shortcut for multiplying by 11 is to multiply by 10 and then add _____ .

Name: _____

105. Carefully compare Monique's likes and dislikes as described here. Write a sentence explaining what all of Monique's likes share.

Monique likes quarrels . . . but not fights. She likes quiet . . . but not silence. She likes quickness . . . but not speed. She likes squares . . . but not rectangles. She likes masquerades . . . but not disguises.

Name: _____

106. Carefully compare Nick's likes and dislikes as described here. Write a sentence explaining what all of Nick's likes share.

Nick likes clocks . . . but not watches. Nick likes tricks . . . but not jokes or magic. Nick likes sticks . . . but not branches. Nick likes snacks . . . but not dessert.

Name: _____

Attributes

107. Carefully compare Betsy's likes and dislikes as described here.
Write a sentence explaining what all of Betsy's likes share.

Betsy likes basketball . . . but not hoops. Betsy likes biscuits . . . but not cookies.
She likes brains . . . but not intelligence, and she likes books . . . but not reading.

Name: _____

Attributes

108. Carefully compare Bobby's likes and dislikes as described here.
Write a sentence explaining what all of Bobby's likes share.

Bobby likes getting letters . . . but not mail. Bobby likes kittens . . . but not cats. He
likes puppies . . . but not dogs, and he likes cattle . . . but not cows.

Name: _____

Attributes

109. Carefully compare Kate's likes and dislikes as described here.
Write a sentence explaining what all of Kate's likes share.

Kate likes tables . . . but not desks. She likes rules . . . but not commands. Kate
likes games . . . but not toys. She also likes magazines . . . but not periodicals, and
roses . . . but not flowers.

Name: _____

Attributes

110. Create your own "likes and dislikes" riddle.

List three or more words that share the same attribute, and three
or more words that are similar in meaning to each of the first
three words you selected, but don't contain the attribute you
identified. When you're ready, pass your paper to a classmate.
Can he or she figure out what attribute you selected?

Name: _____

111. Take a quick look around your classroom, and find ten or more items that begin with the letter D.

Make a list of these items, placing them in alphabetical order.

Name: _____

112. In what ways is clothing like the parts of a building?

You could say that a hat is like a roof, because both are a covering. Draw a line from a clothing word in the left column to the part of the building on the right that it is most like. In a sentence or two, explain what connection you made between these two items.

Clothing	Building Part
hat	window
shoe	doorknob
shirt	carpet
socks	roof
button	floor
eyeglasses	closet
pocket	wall

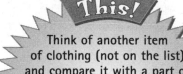

Try This!

Think of another item of clothing (not on the list) and compare it with a part of a building. On a separate page, explain your comparison. Draw a picture to support your explanation.

Name: _____

113. In each *analogy*, or comparison, one word is left out. Complete each analogy by filling in the blank spaces with appropriate words.

a) Back is to front as outside is to _____.

b) Left is to right as west is to _____.

c) Story is to book as _____ is to magazine.

Analogies

Name: _____

114. Complete each analogy by filling in the blank spaces with appropriate words.

a) Kitchen is to cooking as _____ is to _____.

b) Rug is to floor as _____ is to _____.

c) Keyboard is to computer as _____ is to _____.

TiP

Word play games are a great way to improve your vocabulary.

Logic

Name: _____

115. The three statements listed below are all true. However, as they appear now, the third statement cannot be drawn as a conclusion from the two statements above it. Put a check next to the statement that can be concluded from the other two.

_____ All mammals are warm-blooded.

_____ All whales are warm-blooded.

_____ Whales are mammals.

TiP

Even if you don't think you know the answer to a problem, you can sometimes use common sense to arrive at the correct solution.

Logic

Name: _____

116. With a classmate, discuss what is wrong with the conclusion drawn in the third statement from the two above it. Together, come up with a set of true statements that follow this pattern: 1) All A's are B's. 2) All B's are C's. 3) Therefore, all A's are C's.

1) All cars have four wheels.

2) A skateboard has four wheels.

3) Therefore, a skateboard is a car.

Name: _____

117. Using the clues and the list of United States presidents, complete the statements below.

U.S. Presidents

James Madison

Franklin D. Roosevelt

Grover Cleveland

William Henry Harrison

a) _____ was the shortest, standing only 5 feet, 4 inches tall.

b) _____ had the "Baby Ruth" candy bar named after his daughter.

c) _____ died after serving only 32 days in office.

d) _____ was the first president to appear on television.

Clues:

James Madison had no children.

Franklin Delano Roosevelt's only daughter's name was Anne.

William Henry Harrison and James Madison died before TV was invented.

William Henry Harrison stood 5 feet 8 inches tall.

William Henry Harrison's daughters were named Elizabeth, Lucy, Mary, and Anne.

Name: _____

118. What were some of the events that led up to the start of the American Revolution? Place a number from 1 to 4 next to each of the steps below so they appear in chronological order.

_____ In protest of the taxes that were imposed on them, the colonists boycotted British goods.

_____ To help make up for the money they lost during the French and Indian War, the British imposed heavy taxes on many items that the American colonists used all the time.

_____ To protest the tax on tea, the colonist dumped English tea into Boston Harbor—an act that became known as "The Boston Tea Party."

_____ Because of the protests, the British were forced to repeal their taxes—except for the one on tea.

Name: _____

119. Did you know that when you eat vegetables, you are eating different plant parts? Most vegetables come from a plant's root, stem, leaf, seed, or flower. Create a table that matches each of these vegetables to the plant part it comes from.

- carrot
- peas
- celery
- broccoli
- lettuce

TiP

You know a lot more information than you may think! When you come across a test question that you don't know the answer to at first, stay relaxed. Return to that question after you've completed some others. Sometimes the answer will come to you... when you least expect it to!

Name: _____

120. Read the passage below. What period in U.S. history do you think is being described? Explain what details in the passage led you to your conclusion.

Suddenly a male-dominated America was confronted with the spectacle of women auto mechanics, telegraph messengers, elevator operators, and streetcar conductors— and that was not all. They toiled on factor assembly lines, carried ice for iceboxes, plowed fields, and became traffic cops. Women invaded even the sanctuary of the armed forces, about eleven thousand female yeomen enlisting in the navy as clerks and stenographers.

Name: _____

121. Read the passage below. What period in U.S. history do you think is being described? Explain what details in the passage led you to your conclusion.

The skies were darkened . . . The dry soil drifted like snow, drivers had to use their headlights at noon, families stuffed door and window cracks to keep from being choked, livestock died of thirst, and the dust blew farther east and fell into the Atlantic Ocean. Millions of acres of farmland lost their topsoil and thousands of families fled their homes. Most of them headed for California in battered trucks and limping passenger cars, with such furniture and other possessions as they could stuff inside or fasten to the sides and roof.

Prior Knowledge

Name: _____

122. Imagine that your teacher has assigned you to do a research report about these topics: musical instruments, natural disasters, and environmental issues.

Before you head off to the library to begin your research, list five or more words or phrases you might look up in a card catalog, encyclopedia, or online search engine to help you begin your research about each one.

Prior Knowledge

Name: _____

123. Imagine you are on the Internet, trying to research George Washington. After accessing a search engine, you type in the word "Washington."

What are some possible topics, unrelated to what you are trying to find out, that might come up on the computer screen? Write your response in one or more complete sentences.

Prior Knowledge

Name: _____

124. Which of the following reference books would not help you find the square area of the United States? Circle your answer.

- atlas
- almanac
- encyclopedia
- dictionary

Describe how you would go about looking up the square area of the United States in each of the remaining three reference books.

Name: _____

125. Imagine that all you have handy are the following reference books: a dictionary, a set of encyclopedias, an almanac, and an atlas. Which would you use to look up each of the following facts?

a) The year that Mississippi became a state.

b) The states that border Mississippi.

c) The current population of Mississippi.

d) The current governor of Mississippi.

e) How to pronounce *Mississippi*.

Write the letters **a** to **e**. Next to each letter, write the type of reference book you'd use to look up that particular fact.

Name: _____

126. Imagine you are doing some research using a book titled *Rachel Carson: Her Life and Times*. Which section of the book (glossary, bibliography, title page, table of contents, or index) would you use to look up . . .

a) the author of the book *Rachel Carson: Her Life and Times*?

b) the section of the book that describes Carson's childhood?

c) what DDT is? (DDT is a chemical pesticide, banned in 1972, largely because of Carson's writings about how harmful it was to the environment.)

d) specific pages in the book that mention John F. Kennedy and how Rachel Carson affected his presidency?

e) the year the book *Rachel Carson: Her Life and Times* was published?

f) other good sources of information about Rachel Carson?

Write the letters **a** to **f**. Next to each letter, write the part of the book that you'd use to look up that particular piece of information.

Name: _____

127. The Dewey Decimal System for organizing books was devised in 1876 by a librarian named Melvil Dewey. Dewey pretended to be a prehistoric person asking questions about the modern world. He then used this list of questions to create these ten subject categories.

000   General works (encyclopedias, almanacs, etc.)

100   Who am I? (Philosophy and Psychology)

200   Who made me? (Religion)

300   Who are those people over there? (Social Science)

400   How can I make them understand me? (Language)

500   How can I understand the world around me? (Science)

600   How can I use what I know about science? (Applied Science/Technology)

700   How can I enjoy my leisure time? (Fine Arts and Recreation)

800   How can I tell my children about humankind's heroic thoughts and deeds? (Literature)

900   How can I leave a record for people of the future? (History, Geography, Biography)

List the names of five nonfiction books that you have read recently, or that appear on the shelves of your classroom. Using the list above, determine in which category you think each one belongs. List the books in the Dewey Decimal order.

Name: _____

128. List three or more types of information that you have had to memorize at one time or another.

TiP

There's no way around it: Some facts—like the times table, measurement facts, spelling rules, and historic dates need to be memorized.

Name: _____

Memorizing

129. List three or more suggestions you would offer a classmate who is hoping to improve his or her memorization skills.

Name: _____

Memorizing

130. Listen carefully as I read the names of the Great Lakes in order from largest to smallest (based on water surface area). I will read through the list twice. When I'm done, write down as many of the names—ideally in the same order—as you can remember.

Lake Superior, Lake Huron, Lake Michigan, Lake Erie, and Lake Ontario.

Partner
Read these directions to a classmate.

Name: _____

Memorizing

131. Listen carefully as I read the names of the first five presidents of the United States. I will read through the list twice. When I'm done, write down as many of the names—ideally in sequential order—as you can remember.

George Washington, John Adams, Thomas Jefferson, James Madison, and James Monroe.

Partner
Read these directions to a classmate.

Name: _____

Memorizing

132. Listen carefully as I read the names of the first ten presidents of the United States. I will read the list twice. When I'm done, write down as many of the names—ideally in sequential order—as you can remember.

George Washington, John Adams, Thomas Jefferson, James Madison, James Monroe, John Quincy Adams, Andrew Jackson, Martin Van Buren, William Henry Harrison, and John Tyler

Partner
Read these directions to a classmate.

Name: _____

Partner

Read these directions to a classmate.

133. Listen carefully as I read the names of the first thirteen colonies of the United States in the order in which they ratified the Constitution, and thus became a state in the Union. I will read through the list twice. When I'm done, write down as many of the state names—ideally in sequential order—as you can remember.

Delaware, Pennsylvania, New Jersey, Georgia, Connecticut, Massachusetts, Maryland, South Carolina, New Hampshire, Virginia, New York, North Carolina, and Rhode Island

---

Name: _____

Organizing Data

134. Use the center circle of this graphic organizer to describe what it shows. Add an additional appropriate word to each section.

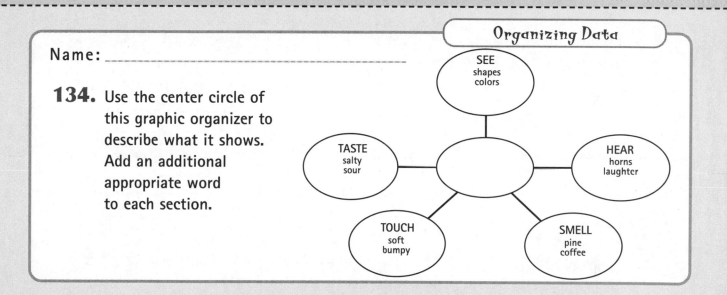

SEE
shapes
colors

TASTE
salty
sour

HEAR
horns
laughter

TOUCH
soft
bumpy

SMELL
pine
coffee

Name: _____

Organizing Data

135. The Venn diagram below shows the results of a survey in which 300 people were asked if they have seen Movie A and/or Movie B. Use the diagram to figure out how many people, of those surveyed, have not seen either movie. Explain your answer, showing how you arrived at it.

Movie Survey Results

Movie A | Movie B

92   28   139

Name: _____

136. Here's an ad like one that actually appeared in a magazine—but there's a math mistake in it! Find the mistake and explain what it is.

Vince's Videos Dept. DE1

Box 2 Turtle Beach, SC 29578

YES. Please do rush my Audience Favorites Video(s). (How Many?)

_____ Audience Favorites Video(s), 45-Minute Show (Item#W159), each only $19.95 plus $3.95 postage & handling.

_____ Audience Favorites Video(s), 90-Minute Show (Item#W160), each only $29.95 plus $4.95 postage & handling (Contains the same material as 45-Minute version, plus an additional hour.)

Enclosed is $_____

CHARGE TO MY CREDIT CARD:
Acct. No. _____
Exp. Date _____

Name _____
Address _____
City _____
State _____ Zip _____

Name: _____

137. Look carefully at the three bar graphs shown below. They each show the exact same data; that is, how many raffle tickets three students at the same school managed to sell. Write a short essay explaining what makes the graphs look so different from one another. In your essay, explain which you would argue is the best representation of the data, and why you think so.

Raffle Ticket Sales

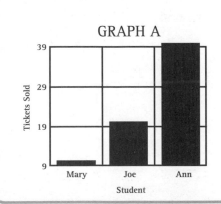

GRAPH A

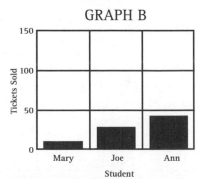

GRAPH B

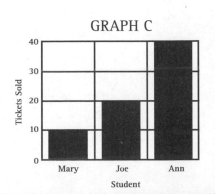

GRAPH C

Name: _____

138. Complete the Venn diagram below by adding two or more additional comparisons to each section of it.

TiP

To figure out what a graph, chart, or diagram is showing, look at its title, and the way the various parts are labeled. This can help you to make connections.

Car and Bicycle Comparison

Cars

Bicycles

Both

four wheels

methods of transportation

two wheels

Name: _____

139. Brainstorm subtopics of the big idea provided on this graphic organizer. Then add another offshoot to each of *those* ideas.

TiP

Don't ignore pictures or diagrams that you see on a test. They often offer clues that will help you solve a problem, or at least help you to understand what is being asked.

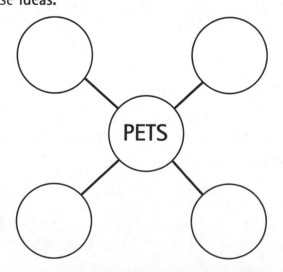

PETS

Name: _____

140. In a short essay, explain the similarities and differences between a chart, a graph, and a graphic organizer.

Name: _____

141. The following word problem is missing some important information that you would need to solve it. Describe what information is missing. Then make up a number fact that would help you solve the problem. Finally, solve the problem using the information that you provided.

Tucker was tuckered out from running. During a school football game, he ran 76 yards to score a touchdown. Then he ran 38 more because it felt so good. By then, he was pooped, but he had to get home for dinner—so he kept going. How many yards did Tucker run in all?

TiP

It's a good idea to know some different terms to express the same concept. For example, in math, "take away," "is how many less than," and "find the difference," all indicate subtraction. Be sure that, no matter which one is used, you'll know exactly what to do!

Name: _____

142. The following word problem contains more information than is actually needed to solve it. Underline the information you need. Then solve the problem. Finally, using some of the information that you did not underline, make up another word problem for a friend to solve.

Franny is a fan of flowers. She paid $4.95 for a dozen daffodils, $2.29 for a bouquet of rhododendrons, and $3.75 for 11 water lilies. She used the $8.42 she had left for allergy medicine. She might love flowers—but her nose doesn't. What was the difference in price between the daffodils and the rhododendrons?

Word Problems

Name: _____

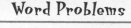

143. This word problem requires you to use more than one computation skill (addition, subtraction, multiplication, or division) in order to solve it. Describe the steps that you must take to solve this problem. After solving it, make up a word problem of your own that requires the use of more than one math operation.

TiP

Drawing a picture or diagram is useful, at times, when trying to solve a problem.

Katy Doodle loves katydids. She carries as many as she can wherever she goes. On last count, she had 3 in each of her 4 pockets, plus 2 stuck in each sock. How many katydids was Katy Doodle carrying in all?

Word Problems

Name: _____

144. This word problem has an answer but no question! Use the information provided to determine the question. Record your answer. Then create a word problem for a friend to solve. Provide only the answer to the problem (as is done here). Be sure that there's enough information given for your friend to figure it out!

Trudy's mother was not happy. Her garden was not turning green as fast as everyone else's. So Trudy decided to spray paint it in time for the official start of spring. She paid a total of $27.50 for 5 cans of green paint. The answer is $5.50. What is the question?

Grammar

Name: _____

145. Explain how the use of commas affects the meaning of these two sentences:

a) Edith Ann, Eddie, and I all went to visit Grandma.

b) Edith, Ann, Eddie, and I all went to visit Grandma.

TiP

Even if you don't love grammar, it's a good idea to be familiar with some of the most common spelling and punctuation errors. Look them up in any good grammar guide. Then find ways to remember not to make those same mistakes!

Grammar

Name: _____

146. Explain how the use of commas affects the meaning of these two sentences:

a) No cameras are allowed in the theater.

b) No, cameras are allowed in the theater.

Grammar

Name: _____

147. Explain how the use of commas affects the meaning of these two sentences:

a) You better call Mom before the store closes.

b) You better call, Mom, before the store closes.

5-Minute Daily Practice: Test Taking Scholastic Professional Books

Name: _____

Grammar

148. Rewrite the following sentences so they are grammatically correct:

    a) Your the fastest runner the coach has ever seen.

    b) Ben and me decided to enter the race together.

    c) We lived in our current apartment for ten years.

    d) To improve your grammar skills, one must learn its rules.

Name: _____

Grammar

149. Rewrite the following sentence so it is punctuated correctly:

    my sister katie is my best friend said eric

Name: _____

Grammar

150. Create an original sentence that follows this grammatical pattern:

    Article-Adjective-Noun-Verb-Adverb

Name: _____

Grammar

151. Write an original declarative sentence, interrogative sentence, imperative sentence, and exclamatory sentence. Label each one.

Name: _____

Grammar

152. Identify each word in the following sentence as either an article, noun, verb, adjective, adverb, pronoun, interjection, conjunction, or preposition:

Hey! I want Aaron to run home and get the other sweater now.

Name: _____

Short Answer

153. Determine the number of days left in the current calendar year. (Include today as one of the days that are left.) Show your work. Beneath your answer, write a short paragraph explaining how you arrived at that solution.

TiP

Always write neatly. It'd be a shame to be marked wrong for an answer on a test, simply because your teacher or the test-grader couldn't read your writing!

Name: _____

Short Answer

154. Determine on what day of the week your birthday will fall five years from now. Show your work. Beneath your answer, write a short paragraph explaining how you arrived at that solution.

Name: _____

Short Answer

155. Write a paragraph explaining how one could figure out the number of seconds there are in a day. Make sure your solution appears within the paragraph that you write.

1, 2, 3...

Short Answer

Name: _____

156. Figure out what year it was a billion seconds ago. Show your work. Beneath your answer, write a short paragraph explaining how you figured it out.

Short Answer

Name: _____

157. Sam Adams, one of America's founding fathers, sometimes told the following story at political meetings.

TiP

When you are asked to answer questions about a passage on a test, sometimes it helps to read the questions before you read the passage. This will give you an idea of the types of information that you will be looking for.

A Story Sam Adams Liked to Tell

A Grecian philosopher, lying asleep upon the grass, awoke when an animal bit him on the palm of his hand. He closed his hand suddenly, as he awoke, and found that he had caught a field mouse. As he examined the little animal, it unexpectedly bit him again. As he dropped it, he thought to himself: "There is no animal, however weak, which cannot defend its own liberty, if only it will fight for it."

Using what you know about the American Revolution, explain what you think the moral of Adams' story was, and why you think he liked telling it so much.

Adapted from *Early American Almanac* by Noreen Banks
People's Bicentennial Commission, 1975.

Name: _____

158. The following story appeared in a textbook that was used in the United States during the 1800s. It will be read aloud twice. On the first reading, listen carefully. As it is read a second time, jot down any notes that you feel might help you when it comes time to answer questions about the story.

Do this with the whole class.

The Boy Rebuked By His Dog

A favorite dog in a farmhouse was standing by his mistress one morning as she prepared her children Eliza and Edmund for school. Eliza had been busy assisting Edmund, who now stood waiting with his hat in his hand, while the mother prepared his sister as fast as possible to go with him.

As it was becoming late, she requested Edmund to fetch their basket, that as soon as she could get his sister ready she might prepare their dinner.

But this negligent and idle boy only gave a sour and surly look, and though he did not really refuse, yet he delayed to obey his mother's command.

"Well, my son," said she, "if you are unwilling to do anything for yourself, how can you expect others will do so much for you? Your Mungo," said she, looking round at the dog, "would bring the basket in a moment, if he only knew how."

As the mother said this, only as a gentle rebuke to her ungrateful son, what was her surprise to see the dog hasten to the closet, take the basket from behind the door and with an air of joy and delight, come and put it down by her side?

Let those children who are unwilling to assist their parents, teachers and others, even when it is for their interest to do so, blush and be rebuked by the example of this noble dog.

Now, using what you've heard and the notes you've taken, write a paragraph summarizing the story "The Boy Rebuked By His Dog." In your summary, include the answers to these questions:

a) What did the mother ask Edmund to fetch her, as she helped the sister get ready for school?

b) What was the dog's name?

c) Based on what you've heard, what do you think the word *rebuked* means?

d) How would you describe the moral of this story?

From *The School Reader: Third Book* by Charles W. Sanders; originally published by Mark H. Newman, New York, 1843. As reprinted in *Early American School Books*, Chandler Press, 1988.

Name: _____

Short Answer

159. American cartoonist Rube Goldberg is known for his kooky drawings of complex contraptions designed to perform simple tasks. For example, shown below is one based on his idea for a fancy pencil sharpener. To start it working, all someone has to do is open the window! As best as you can, describe in your own words how this invention works.

TiP

Sometimes on a test you may be asked to pick one short answer or one essay question out of five (or two out of four, or whatever!) Be sure you don't select any more than you have been told to!

Name: _____

Essay

160. Using the same materials (you don't need to use them all!) included in the contraption shown in #159, write an essay describing your own Rube Goldberg-like invention for closing the window— without someone ever touching the window!

TiP

To write an essay in a short period of time, it helps to organize your thoughts by creating a brief outline first.

Name: _____

Essay

161. Write an outline for a persuasive essay about why kids should or should not wear uniforms to school. In your outline, include a topic sentence, at least three or more supporting arguments backing up your opinion, and a summarization of the major points you wish to make.

Name: _____

Essay

162. Write an outline for a short essay evaluating whether or not you agree with the following maxim: "Stubborn people are never so much so as when they are wrong." Be sure to provide examples to prove your point.

Name: _____

Essay

163. In an essay, you may be asked to compare, summarize, analyze, evaluate, or explain. In a short essay, explain what would distinguish the focus of essays that asked you to do each of these.

TiP

Writing serves one of three purposes: to entertain, to inform, or to persuade. Whenever you are about to read or write an essay, be sure you know which purpose the essay is supposed to serve.

Name: _____

Essay

164. In your own words, explain the meaning of the following maxim: "Nature has wisely furnished us with two ears and one tongue; a most useful lesson if rightly applied."

Name: _____

Essay

165. A proverb is a short statement meant to provide a bit of advice or wisdom. For example, two fairly well-known proverbs are "Haste makes waste," and "Look before you leap." In a short essay, explain what each means and compare them. In what ways are these words of advice similar? How, if at all, do they differ?

Name: _____

166. A compound machine is one that is made up of more than one simple machine (such as a lever, wedge, inclined plane, pulley, screw, or wheel and axle). Select or make up an original compound machine. In a short essay, describe how this machine works, and which simple machines it is constructed from.

Name: _____

167. Write a set of directions describing how to get from your classroom to another place in your school or neighborhood. In your instructions, use landmarks and words like *right, left, straight, north, south, east,* and *west,* but do not mention the destination. Read the directions to a classmate. Can he or she determine what the final destination is?

TIP
To help you remember what you hear, try visualizing the meanings of the words.

Name: _____

168. Choose someone to read aloud the following to the class:

Do this with the whole class.

We're going to play a game called "Buzz." It was played in pioneer days to help students practice and improve their multiplication skills. Listen carefully to the rules: To begin, each student selects a number between 3 and 12 and writes it on a sheet of paper. This is your "buzz number." As we go around the room, we will count up from 1, with this exception: If the number you would say when it is your turn is a multiple of your "buzz number," hold up your paper and call out "buzz!" If you forget, or mistakenly call out "buzz" at the wrong time, you are out of the game. The last student remaining wins.

Name: _____

169. Close your eyes and listen carefully to the following set of directions. When you've heard the entire set, determine which way you'd be facing if you were to carry them out. You are facing north. You head in that direction a quarter-mile, and then head west. After five blocks you turn to your right. What direction are you facing now?

Read these directions to a classmate.

Name: _____

170. Close your eyes and listen carefully to the following set of directions. When you've heard the entire set, determine which way you'd be facing if you were to carry them out. You are facing south. You head in that direction until you reach a stop sign, then turn to your left. What direction are you facing now?

Read these directions to a classmate.

Name: _____

171. Close your eyes and listen carefully to the following set of directions. When you've heard the entire set, determine which direction you'd be facing if you were to carry them out. You are facing west. You do a 180° turn so you are facing the opposite direction, then make a 90° turn to your left. You now do another 180° turn. What direction are you facing now?

Read these directions to a classmate.

Name: _____

172. Sit with your eyes closed as you imagine yourself following this list of instructions:

Standing straight and tall, place your left hand on your right funny bone, and your right hand on your forehead. Then cross your legs and lean over as far as you can.

Now stand up and demonstrate the position in which you would be standing, if you'd been following these directions as they were read.

Read these directions to a classmate.

Name: _____

173. Sit with your eyes closed as you imagine yourself following this list of instructions:

Stand straight and tall, facing the front of the classroom. Then turn to your right as you raise your right hand as high as you can. Place your left hand on your left hip, your right hand on your left foot, and your left hand on the opposite ankle.

Now stand up and demonstrate the position in which you would be standing, if you'd been following these directions as they were read.

Partner
Read these directions to a classmate.

Name: _____

174. Sit with your eyes closed as you imagine yourself following this list of instructions:

Stand straight and tall, and wrinkle your nose. Shake your wrists. Then move your right arm as though you were pledging allegiance to the flag. Lean your head to the right. Bend your right knee, and lean your head the opposite way.

Now stand up and demonstrate the position in which you would be standing, if you'd been following these directions as they were read.

Partner
Read these directions to a classmate.

Name: _____

175. Make up a set of Simon Says–like instructions for a friend to follow. Write them down. Then read them to a partner. See if your partner can figure out what pose or position he or she would wind up in when finished.

Name: _____

176. Sit with your eyes closed as you imagine yourself following this list of instructions:

Write down the word PET. Change the E to an I. Add an S before the P, and an L after the P. Now write down the word you wind up with after following this set of directions, and use it in a sentence.

Partner
Read these directions to a classmate.

Name: _____

Listening

177. Sit with your eyes closed as you imagine yourself following this list of instructions:

Write down the word CHANGE. Change the HA to RI. Delete the first and last letter in the new word that you arrive at. Now write down the word you wind up with after following this set of directions, and use it in a sentence.

Partner

Read these directions to a classmate.

Name: _____

Listening

178. Sit with your eyes closed as you imagine yourself following this list of instructions:

Write down the word PROP. Change the first letter to an E and move it to the end of the word. Change the P to a B, and add an S at the end. Now write down the word you wind up with after following this set of directions, and use it in a sentence.

Partner

Read these directions to a classmate.

Name: _____

Listening

179. Sit with your eyes closed as you imagine yourself following this list of instructions:

Write down the word CARE. Delete the E, and add an S at both the beginning and end of the word. Then change the R to a B. Now write down the word you wind up with after following this set of directions, and use it in a sentence.

Partner

Read these directions to a classmate.

Name: _____

Listening

180. Make up a "Create-a-Word"-like set of instructions for a friend to follow. Write them down. Then read them to a partner. See if your partner can figure out what word he or she should wind up with when finished. Have your partner use the word in a sentence.

Answers

1-5. Answers will vary.

6-7. As written, it is unclear which shape should be placed above, below, to the right, or to the left of the others.

8. The paper can be folded first horizontally and then vertically; vertically and then horizontally; or on a diagonal first (if it is a square sheet).

9. Answers will vary.

10. The decoded message reads either: DID YOU KNOW WHICH LETTER TO CROSS OUT FIRST HERE? *or* HOW DID YOU KNOW WHICH LETTER TO CROSS OUT FIRST? (It depends on which letter students begin with.)

11-12. Answers will vary.

13. A, C, and E should have a ✓; B, D, and F should be darkened.

14. 18, 72, 234, and 243 should have an X; 129 should have a funny face in it.

15. Arctic, Pacific, Indian, and Atlantic should have an X beside them; Antarctica, Asia, North America, Europe, Australia, South America, and Africa should have a ✓.

16. a

17. Answers will vary.

18. Pencils go down at 9:42.

19. Pencils go down at 10:38.

20-21. a) knot; c) knot; d) knot

22. The result should be a square sheet of paper with a 4-pointed, star-shaped hole in its center.

23. Students should have followed only steps A, B, and L.

24. (1) Mercury, (2) Venus, (3) Earth, (4) Mars, (5) Jupiter, (6) Saturn, (7) Uranus, (8) Neptune, (9) Pluto

25. (1) My, (2) Very, (3) Educated, (4) Mother, (5) Just, (6) Served, (7) Us, (8) Nine, (9) Pizzas

26-27. Answers will vary.

28. ROY G. BIV

29. Hour: 4
Week: 6
Year: 8
Second: 2
Decade: 9
Day: 5
Month: 7
Millisecond: 1
Century: 10
Minute: 3

30. Annually: ⅢⅢ //
Semiannually: ⅢⅢ /
Quarterly: ⅢⅢ
Centennially: ⅢⅢ ///
Millennially: ⅢⅢ ////
Semiweekly: //
Weekly: ///
Daily: /
Monthly: ////

31. Quadruplets: G
Nonuplets: B
Decaplets: A
Quintuplets: F
Septuplets: D
Twins: I
Sextuplets: E
Triplets: H
Octuplets: C

32. Decagon: H
Dodecagon: J
Triangle: A
Quadrilateral: B
Pentagon: C
Octagon: F
Hendecagon: I
Nonagon: G
Hexagon: D
Heptagon: E

33. Quaternary: 4
Denary: 10
Septenary: 7
Secondary: 2
Quinary: 5
Nonary: 9
Tertiary: 3
Primary: 1
Octonary: 8
Senary: 6

34. Tri-: three
Quad-: four
Oct-: eight
Deca-: ten
Cent-: one hundred

35. 1. 1 tablespoon
2. 4 teaspoons
3. 1 ounce
4. 1/2 cup

36. A. 1/2 pint
B. 1 1/2 cups
C. 14 ounces
D. 3/4 quart

37. I. 1/8 mile
II. 4 yards
III. 40 inches
IV. 2 1/2 feet

38. Kilo-: 1,000
Hecto-: 100
Deca-: 10
Deci-: 1/10
Centi-: 1/100
Milli-: 1/1000

39. The fractions that continue the pattern are 6/12, 7/14, 8/16. These fractions, which all equal one-half, are created with numerators that begin at 1, and increase by one each time.

40. The numbers that continue the pattern are 42, 56, 72. In this series, 4 is added to the first number, 6 is added to the second number, 8 is added to the third, and so on.

41. The numbers that continue the pattern are 36, 49, 64. These numbers represent, in sequence, each number multiplied by itself: 1x1, 2x2, 3x3, 4x4, and so on.

42. Answers will vary.

43. It would take about 12 oranges to produce 1 quart of orange juice.

44. Milliliter: A teaspoon of water; Gram: A dollar bill; Kilogram: A sack of oranges; Kilometer: An airport landing strip; Liter: A bottle of soda; Milligram: A grain of sand; Millimeter: The thickness of a penny; Centimeter: The width of a fingernail; Meter: The length of a baseball bat

45. Approximately: a) 19 cm; b) 330 g; c) 350 ml

46. Answers will vary.

47. a) cube; d) cube; e) cube; A shape must have six squares, and two of them must stick out on opposite sides to form the cube's top and bottom.

48. microbe, microcosm, microfilm, microscope, microwave

49. biology, criminology, ecology, genealogy, technology

50-53. Answers will vary.

54. Considerable (a significant amount)

55. Answers will vary.

56. Tepid (lukewarm)

57. Answers will vary.

58. One rephrasing: The food lover was sorry, and promised to control himself better when gently criticized for his excessive eating and huge appetite.

59. One rephrasing: Sheldon was shocked at his ill-tempered grandmother's loud complaints over Sheldon's wisecracking joking.

60. pneumo: lung; ultra-microscopic: extra small; silico: silicon-related; volcano: referring to particles found in a volcano; coni: dust; osis: diseased condition

61. a) drizzle b) clouds c) rain d) wind

62. Estuary; all the others are people-made places where animals are kept confined for protection or other reasons.

63. a) ramp; b) bottle opener; c) well; d) swivel chair; e) doorstop; f) egg beater

64. Answers will vary.

65. be/bee; ode/owed; two/too; thrown/throne; lone/loan; patience/patients; here/hear; residents/residence; cents/sense

66. do (dew); you (ewe); would (wood); I (eye); in (inn); you'll (Yule); read (reed); (ore, oar); who's (whose); meet (meat); know (no)

67-68. Answers will vary.

69. Answers will vary. One meaning of each word has to do with baseball.

70. Homonyms have the same pronunciation and often the same spelling, but different meanings. Homographs have the same spelling but different meanings and possibly different pronunciations.

71.

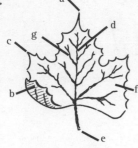

72. Your <u>absence</u> was <u>sorely</u> <u>missed</u> at the <u>school's</u> <u>holiday</u> <u>celebration</u> yesterday.

73. sheriff; fascinating; legal

74. I cannot wait to see you for your birthday. That will be so excellent!

75-76. Results will vary.

77. A person who is able to contribute something to the world is a fortunate person, and each of us should be able at least to "brighten the corner" where we are. –Charles Schultz, cartoonist

78. I have a dream that one day this nation will rise up and live out the true meaning of its creed: "We hold these truths to be self-evident; that all men are created equal." –Martin Luther King, Jr., civil rights leader; The letter substitute pattern used here is the alphabet, but backward: A = Z, B = Y, and so on.

79. E = 7; N = 6; O = 4; T = 9; W = 3.

80. 7; 10; 5

81. 3 x 11 + 4 = 36 + 1

82. 27

83. 8

84. C

85. B

86. C

87. B

88. D

89. D

90. A

91. D

92. 5 x (7 + 4) = (10 ÷ 2) + (25 x 2). [Given order of operations, the second two sets of parentheses are not technically required.]

93. True

94. True

95. False

96. True

97. False

98. True

99. 2

100. 3

101. 8

102. 4; 4

103. 2

104. the number

105. Monique likes words containing a *qu.*

106. Nick likes words ending in *cks.*

107. Betsy likes words that start with *B.*

108. Bobby likes words with a *double letter* in them, or only *two-syllable* words.

109. Kate likes words containing a *silent e,* or words that end in *es.*

110-111. Answers will vary.

112. hat/roof; shoe/floor; shirt/wall; socks/carpet; button/doorknob; eyeglasses/windows; pocket/closet.

113. a) inside; b) east; c) article

114. Answers will vary.

115. All whales are warm-blooded.

116. Answers will vary.

117. a) James Madison; b) Grover Cleveland; c) William Henry Harrison; d) Franklin D. Roosevelt

118. 2; 1; 4; 3

119. carrot/root; celery/stem; lettuce/leaf; broccoli/flower; peas/seed

120. The passage describes the start of World War I, circa 1917, when items like telegraphs, streetcars and ice-boxes were more common.

121. The passage describes the Dust Bowl of the 1930s.

122-123. Answers will vary.

124. dictionary

125. a) an encyclopedia; b) an atlas; c) an almanac; d) an almanac; e) a dictionary

126. a) title page; b) table of contents; c) glossary; d) index; e) title page; f) bibliography

127-129. Answers will vary.

130–133. Results will vary.

134. The chart shows nouns and adjectives that relate to each of the five senses.

135. 41 people surveyed did not see either movie.

136. There are two possible answers. The 90-minute show could contain the same material as the 45-minute version plus an additional 45 minutes, not an additional hour. Or the tape might be 105 minutes long, not 90 minutes, because 45 minutes plus an additional hour equals 105 minutes.

137. Graph C is the best representation of the data. The numbers on the Y axis of Graph A make it look like Ann has sold many more raffle tickets than the other two students, and the numbers on the Y axis of Graph B make it look like there is only a small difference in the numbers sold. Only Graph C starts at 0 and rises in increments that fairly reflect the information provided.

138-140. Answers will vary.

141. The missing information is the distance between where Tucker got tired and his home.

142. The price difference between the daffodils and rhododendrons is $2.66 ($4.95-$2.29). Answers to the second part of the problem will vary.

143. Katy Doodle was carrying (3 x 4) + (2 x 2), or 16 katydids. Answers to the second part of the problem will vary.

144. The question is: What was the cost of one can of green paint? Answers to the second part of the problem will vary.

145. The first sentence involves three people; the second sentence includes four.

146. In the first sentence cameras are not allowed in the theater; in the second sentence they are.

147. In the first sentence, Mom is the one being called; in the second sentence it is recommended that Mom call.

148. a) You're (*or* You are) the fastest runner the coach has ever seen. b) Ben and I decided to enter the race together. c) We have lived in our current apartment for ten years. d) To improve your grammar skills, you must learn its rules, *or* To improve one's grammar skills, one must learn its rules.

149. The corrected sentence should read: "My sister Katie is my best friend," said Eric.

150-151. Answers will vary.

152. Interjection, Pronoun, Verb, Noun, Preposition, Verb, Noun, Conjunction, Verb, Article, Adjective, Noun, Adverb.

153-154. Answers will vary.

155. Explanations will vary. There are 86,400 seconds in a 24-hour day.

156. Answers and explanations will vary. A billion seconds = approximately 11,574 years.

157. Answers will vary.

158. a) basket b) Mungo c) reprimanded d) Answers will vary.

159-167. Answers will vary.

168. Results will vary.

169. north

170. east

171. south

172-175. Results will vary.

176. The final word is *split.* Student sentences will vary.

177. The final word is *ring.* Student sentences will vary.

178. The final word is *robes.* Student sentences will vary.

179. The final word is *scabs.* Student sentences will vary.

180. Answers will vary.